**C. S. BARBER**
P. O. Box #50344
Jax Beach, FL 32240-0344
904/246-2310

# Daily Lessons Received at 'Akká January 1908

# Daily Lessons Received at 'Akká January 1908

HELEN S. GOODALL
*and*
ELLA GOODALL COOPER

BAHÁ'Í PUBLISHING TRUST
Wilmette, Illinois 60091

Copyright © 1979 by the
National Spiritual Assembly of the
Bahá'ís of the United States

World Rights Reserved

Revised Edition

**Library of Congress Cataloging in Publication Data**

Goodall, Helen S
  Daily lessons received at 'Akká, January 1908.

  Original ed. published in 1908 under title:
Daily lessons received at Acca, January 1908.
  Includes bibliographical references.
  1. Abd ul-Bahá ibn Bahá Ulláh, 1844–1921.
2. Goodall, Helen S.  3. Cooper, Ella Goodall,
1879–1951.  4. Bahaism—Biography.  5. Bahaism—
Prayer-books and devotions—English.  I. Cooper,
Ella Goodall, 1879–1951.  II. Title.
BP393.G66    1979    297'.89    79-19806
ISBN 0-87743-135-3

Design by John Solarz

Printed in the United States of America

10  9  8  7  6  5  4  3  2  1

## CONTENTS

| | |
|---|---|
| *Foreword* | vii |
| Introduction | 3 |
| Arrival at 'Akká | 6 |
| The Household | 8 |
| Morning Service | 12 |
| The Mashriqu'l-Adhkár | 14 |
| Feast | 15 |
| Sacrifice | 17 |
| Accidental Happenings | 20 |
| The Incident of the Departure of Mírzá Asadulláh from Haifa at the Time of the Disturbance in 1905 | 23 |
| Bahá'í Argument Against the Belief of the Naturalists Regarding the Essence of God or the Reality of Creation | 26 |
| Essence of the Material Creation | 31 |
| Evil Thoughts | 35 |
| Automatic Writing | 37 |
| Memorial Service | 41 |
| Journey of the Israelites | 45 |
| Miracles | 48 |
| Exile of Bahá'u'lláh | 51 |
| Knowing God Through His Manifestation of Himself | 53 |
| The Power of God | 55 |
| Story of Badí' | 57 |
| Inscription on the Greatest Name Stone | 62 |
| Pronunciation of Bahá'o'lláh | 66 |
| Meetings | 67 |
| A Message Sent by 'Abdu'l-Bahá | 68 |
| The Picture of Bahá'u'lláh | 69 |
| Symbolic Picture | 71 |

*Appendices*
   I Tablet to Mrs. Ella Goodall Cooper ............ 77
   II Tablet to Mrs. Ella Goodall Cooper ............ 84
   III Tablet Predicting the "Tests" of
      San Francisco ............................. 88
   IV Portions of Tablets Sent by 'Abdu'l-Bahá ........ 90
*Notes* ............................................ 93

FOREWORD

Before there were Bahá'í books, pamphlets, periodicals—before there were, properly speaking, Bahá'í administrative institutions; before 'Abdu'l-Bahá had made His historic voyage to America; before Shoghi Effendi transmitted to the English speakers of the world his own sensitive and authoritative translations of the Writings central to the Bahá'í Faith—there were Bahá'ís in America. On what spiritual food did they subsist? Ever since the announcement had been made at the World Parliament of Religions in 1893 concerning the spiritual sanctity of Bahá'u'lláh, Americans began to explore the new Revelation. Some Persian Bahá'ís came from the Holy Land about that time to give lessons in the Bahá'í Faith in New York and Chicago. The first pilgrimage to 'Akká and Haifa, in 1898, was followed by a steady and ever-increasing stream of Americans intent on hearing the Faith expounded by 'Abdu'l-Bahá, Whom Bahá'u'lláh had designated Center of the Covenant. The pilgrims, on their return to the United States and Canada, conveyed their ardor, enkindled at the feet of the Master, to their questing compatriots. They did it by word of mouth, by private letter, by widely circulated and continually copied and recopied letters, descriptions, journals, and accounts that went from hand to hand. Sometimes they published their little books and pamphlets, and, when the Bahá'í Publishing Society (predecessor of the present Bahá'í Publishing Trust) was established in 1902, these travelers' accounts constituted an important part of its output.

But infinitely more important than such publications were the Tablets or letters that 'Abdu'l-Bahá sent to the North American pilgrims. He maintained a continuous correspondence with these early believers, who welcomed the Tablets and eagerly, reverently shared them with their friends—by the same means, informal and formal, by which their personal experiences as pilgrims had been shared. The Tablets were written in Persian and were translated into English either in the Holy Land or in America by Persian believers and teachers.

One of the translators of these Tablets was the Master's grandson, Shoghi Effendi, destined by 'Abdu'l-Bahá's Will and Testament to become the Guardian of the Cause of God. There came to be, even before Shoghi Effendi's accession to the Guardianship, a strong sense of the difference between official, authoritative expressions of the thoughts of Bahá'u'lláh and 'Abdu'l-Bahá, on the one hand, and the informal reminiscences of travelers, on the other—of travelers eager to capture the precious words uttered by the Master as He taught the pilgrims—for He always taught; at tea, at lunch, on walks, on expeditions of mercy to the poor, He taught by deeds as well as words. Every minute of the pilgrims' day was a lesson, sometimes concealed to all but the truly sensitive, sometimes apparent to the least gifted. Clearly, in the "pilgrims' notes" (as they came to be called) there was necessarily involved the fallibility of each pilgrim's memory and interpretive capacity. There was a danger that a sentence in a letter, dictated in response to a very particular question, might be generalized far beyond the case to which it was addressed, or that an oral lesson adapted and filtered by the needs of the hearer, become the basis of a doctrine that, emanating from 'Abdu'l-Bahá, would be seen as binding on all believers. Precisely this had happened in Islám; the Traditions, or Ḥadiths—that is, the sayings of Muḥammad as reported by His disciples—had come to represent, for the majority of Muslims, an authority second only to that of the Qur'án itself.

Bahá'u'lláh Himself had made it clear that, as Shoghi Effendi put it in a letter written on his behalf, "only those things that have been revealed in the form of Tablets have a binding power over the friends. Hearsays may be matters of interest but can in no way claim authority." (*Bahá'í News*, no. 125 [May 1939], 6). Shoghi Effendi was particularly vigilant in this matter and repeatedly warned the friends against accepting hearsay as binding on anyone except him who had heard the Master with his own ears. However that may be, what can be more thrilling, short of the immediate experience, than hearing or reading the account in a pilgrim's own words of his reception in the loving arms of the Master? Who can tire of the description of those penetrating eyes, that warm and merry laughter, the wise brow, the wisps of hair escaping from the confining turban? Surely pilgrims' notes are not binding on us; they cannot be adduced as proof of anything; they cannot provide the basis of a serious, critical analysis of Bahá'í teachings—though the temptation to use them so is sometimes nearly irresistible!; but the sense of 'Abdu'l-Bahá's presence, His quintessential courtesy, His tenderness,

His occasional severity, His powers of intellect and concentration—all these are infinitely precious to Bahá'ís, every one of whom is in love with the Master.

---

The account of the pilgrimage of Mrs. Helen S. Goodall and her daughter, Mrs. Ella Goodall Cooper, is among the earliest of the published descriptions of life with the Master, in His household.

Mrs. Goodall and her daughter Ella (not yet married), were attracted to the Faith at the same time. They lived, at the turn of the century, in Oakland and San Francisco, when Lua Getsinger was teaching at Mrs. Phoebe Hearst's home. It was after Mrs. Getsinger had left the region that a niece of Mrs. Hearst's and friend of Ella's told Ella and her mother about the Prophet Who lived in the Holy Land. Both mother and daughter were so fired with the desire to know more that they went to New York City, where they received more informed instruction in the Faith than was available in San Francisco. At this time (1898) Mrs. Hearst, on the first American pilgrimage, cabled a young friend in New York City to join her in the Holy Land and to invite Ella Goodall to accompany her. Young Miss Goodall was delighted to accept and, after securing the permission of 'Abdu'l-Bahá, left for Haifa. Mrs. Goodall was not well enough at that time to undertake so arduous a journey, and so returned to California.

In the meantime, a strong nucleus of believers had formed in the Bay Area, of which Helen Goodall became one of the principal animating forces. She had her chance to go on pilgrimage in 1908 with Ella (now Mrs. George Cooper, married since 1905), for a two-week sojourn in the prison home of 'Abdu'l-Bahá. The Master was still under government surveillance; the Young Turks' revolution had not yet ended His imprisonment. But that Prison was a haven of beauty and freedom, compared with the world outside. The present book is, of course, the outcome of that pilgrimage.

Simple, unstudied, direct, almost without form, it consists of descriptions, anecdotes, questions put to the Master, with the answers He gave, the record of lessons given not only by 'Abdu'l-Bahá, but also by that gifted teacher, Hájí Mírzá Haydar-'Alí. There are also appendices with Tablets from the Master to Mrs. Goodall and to Mrs. Cooper. There is an almost severe economy of expression: no concern for the graceful transition, but rather an abrupt turning of attention to the next matter of concern. This lack of "style" turns out to be the best possible style: it breathes the awareness of the preciousness of the lessons learned, the value of the experiences and observations of the two pilgrims; no time is lost getting to the central thought. A sort of sober ecstasy pervades these pages—no purple prose, no effusions. The flame burns pure.

But, lest you forget—these are just pilgrims' notes.

It would not be appropriate to recount in full the lives of these remarkable women after the pilgrimage of 1908. But the chapter in O. Z. Whitehead's *Some Early Bahá'ís of the West* ("Helen Goodall and Ella Cooper," pp. 21–34) is well worth reading for the sequel. It will suffice here to say that after services of fundamental importance to the establishment of the infant Faith in the United States (not the least of which were contributed to the erection of the House of Worship in Wilmette), Mrs. Goodall died in 1922, her physical vigor having entered into a rapid decline after the passing of the Master. Mrs. Cooper was a loyal and energetic helper of the Guardian until the death of her husband, Dr. George Cooper, in July 1951; she died four days after.

HOWARD GAREY

# Daily Lessons Received at 'Akká January 1908

INTRODUCTION

During our visit of two weeks in the "White City" we shared with 'Abdu'l-Bahá the prison life, but we were in the Home of God. There one is indeed made to feel that he represents and is a part of the whole Bahá'í Kingdom, that the Divine Love poured out upon him from that Spiritual Fountain is for all the believers in the world; but also he must realize that his responsibility increases in proportion to the favors and blessings showered upon him, not only toward God the Bestower of the blessings and 'Abdu'l-Bahá through Whom they flow, but toward all humanity; for in accepting this sweet Water of Life so freely given, it becomes incumbent upon him to give in his turn—all that his capacity will hold; and the more he is favored the greater will be the service expected of him. It is to be thus fitted for higher endeavor that the souls are permitted to make the Pilgrimage, and not because of their deserts.

'Abdu'l-Bahá is no respecter of persons—(His own Personality is entirely in abeyance) and to Him one believer is the same as another. His Love embraces each and all as God's children and needy members of the human race.

In His presence, one gains some realization of the Divine Wisdom required to establish the Kingdom.

Considering that the hearts of the people must first be turned to God (and this depends upon their own desire and choice), and that constant training is necessary to keep the souls in the Straight Path, one understands that only the Power of God could accomplish this Great Work, and also that His chosen Instrument for the purpose must be perfect—not only in qualities, but in wisdom and judgment.

In this connection, what an inspiring thought it is to feel that the early believers have also been chosen by 'Abdu'l-Bahá to serve side by side with Him—during His Lifetime—have been granted the inestimable privilege of becoming real pioneers in the arduous and glorious task of establishing the Kingdom of God in the hearts of men!

'Abdu'l-Bahá's instructions were given to us each day at luncheon. Greeting us with a few words in English, He always summoned us Himself to His bountifully spread table. Besides this material and spiritual food, which we received daily from His Hand, we were privileged to learn many beautiful lessons by watching His daily life. He is indeed the living Exemplar of the truth of Bahá'u'lláh's teaching that "Guidance hath ever been by words, but at *this time* it is by *deeds*—that is, all pure deeds must appear from the temple of man, because all are partners in words, but pure and holy deeds belong especially to Our friends."[1]

His most simple act is full of significance, containing the seed of great teaching. If He never spoke one word to the pilgrims, the only lesson necessary would be His daily life.

And so we have called this little book *Daily Lessons*, meaning the name to embrace both the direct oral instruction and that conveyed by the "pure and holy deeds" of every hour and moment of His Glorious Existence.

# ARRIVAL AT 'AKKÁ

Having first called to see Rúhá Khánum and Madam Asadulláh in Haifa, we arrived at 'Akká at noon January 4th.

As we drove through the streets of the prison city, Mírzá Munír-i Zayn and another believer joined us and walked by the side of the carriage, but without speaking.

We were met at the gate by Mírzá Asadulláh and other men believers who conducted us through the inner court to the long flight of stone steps leading to the third story. At the top we were met by Madame Yazdí (Ridváníyyih, a niece of 'Abdu'l-Bahá who was then visiting there), who showed us to our room. Then dear Munavvar Khánum came with her cordial greeting and announced that 'Abdu'l-Bahá would be with us in a few moments.

He came at once, the joyous ring of His voice reaching us even before we saw Him, calling, "Welcome! Welcome! I am glad you are here!" and adding to His warm, strong handclasp the greater welcome of His wonderful eyes and heavenly smile. He made us sit down with Him and immediately asked about the American believers, of those in London and Paris, and also about our California believers. When we mentioned those who had sent Him special greeting, His beautiful face beamed with happiness.

He asked about our long journey and said, "Those who go in search of the North Pole count as nothing the hardships endured, and although you have come here in the winter when it is cold and the way a little difficult, yet you count the journey as nothing. Those having this Visit as their goal will bear any hardship for the sake of attaining."

## THE HOUSEHOLD

One can only feel but never hope to describe the spiritual atmosphere which surrounds 'Abdu'l-Bahá and the members of His Holy Household. The favored visitor is so quickly enveloped in this subtle Harmony that he is conscious of living in a new element, of breathing a different air from that of the outside world, of being immersed in a perfect Ocean of Divine Love which submerges all his human selfishness for the time being, calling forth and sustaining every spiritual quality of which he is possessed. This effect is produced by the Presence of 'Abdu'l-Bahá, and preserved by those holy souls who revolve around Him.

The members of the Holy Household are:

'Abdu'l-Bahá.

Bahíyyih Khánum, His sister, "The Greatest Holy Leaf."
Munírih Khánum, His wife, "The Brilliant Leaf."
Díá'íyyih Khánum, His eldest daughter, married to Mírzá Hádí. Their three children—Shoghi (boy), Rúhangíz (girl), Mihrangíz (girl).
Rúhá Khánum, His daughter, married to Mírzá Jalál. One child—Maryam (girl).
Túbá Khánum, His daughter, married to Mírzá

Muḥsin. Their three children—Rúḥí (boy), T͟hurayyá (girl), Suhayl (boy).

Munavvar K͟hánum, His youngest daughter, unmarried. All her time is devoted to serving 'Abdu'l-Bahá personally, sharing the superintendence of domestic affairs with the Greatest Holy Leaf and interpreting for the American and English pilgrims.

The Holy Family is served in turn by a score of women, boys, and girls who are dependent upon 'Abdu'l-Bahá's bounty. Some of them are orphans of Persian Martyrs, to whom He offers a home; others are there by their own will, having begged for the privilege of serving. One serves at the house in Haifa, while her daughter is being educated by 'Abdu'l-Bahá, and so on. All seem to realize and appreciate fully the blessing of living under the same roof with Him, and all service is cheerfully and lovingly rendered.

One might easily imagine the daily life of a family of prisoners—even a Holy Family—as sad and depressing to the visitor but, strange to say, in the "Most Great Prison" quite the reverse is the case. Although absolute regularity of living is not possible—nearly every domestic event being subject to the rise of unexpected circumstances—the calm serenity of those beautiful people is never broken. They pursue their daily tasks, render their sweet service, make their little sacrifices, teach their children—and play with them, too—in short, carry on, under the most extraordinary circumstances, a perfect ideal of human family life. One never hears complaint of hard conditions, only a calm acceptance of God's Will and

Wisdom in every little happening, and a sure understanding of the future blessings which will be the fruit of their present patience, blessings for all the people of the world.

Although each individual, from the youngest servant to the Greatest Holy Leaf, is constantly on guard, no parade is made of their watchfulness. Not even the creak of a distant door or a strange footfall escapes their attentive ears, yet the visitor is never reminded that he is the cause of anxiety. When it becomes necessary to move the whole supper table suddenly into another room to escape the observation of the Turkish callers, it is done with a quiet smile and no hint of inconvenience. How obvious and easy it would be to impress the sensitive pilgrim with their daily martyrdom and the constant strain of their precarious position. That they do just the contrary is another lesson to us!

Were it not for the close proximity of the barracks and its guards, one would never realize that he was visiting a Turkish prison.

Another delight to the visitor is the discovery of their spontaneous and charming humor. They make merry over every little jest, extracting all the laughter possible from it, and encourage one another to see the bright side of all things, thus distracting their minds from the tragic side of their existence. 'Abdu'l-Bahá Himself seemed to come so close to us in His playful moods. With a merry twinkle in His eye, He would ask Miss Jack how she liked being on the roll of the prisoners (she is to remain there a year to teach English).[2] When she answered that she would like to be written down as "the woman who had just found her freedom," He laughed with the rest, and was highly pleased that she responded to Him in the same tone. Never have we heard more joyous laughter than in that Household.

Every day 'Abdu'l-Bahá came to our door and called us to His table, which was bountifully spread with material and spiritual food, saying in English, "Come here, come here, sit down, sit down. How are you—very well?" and when we answered, "We are very well," He said in Persian, "Very good, very good; it makes me happy to sit at table with you, because you are the servants of Bahá'u'lláh." We replied that *He* made us happy. He said, "Very good, I am glad you are here. It makes Me rejoice when I see you, for I love you very much."

'Abdu'l-Bahá's perfectly natural manner indicates the entire absence of self-consciousness, and throughout the Household there is absolute simplicity, a constant service, and all the members take a common-sense view of all things.

When emotion is shown, 'Abdu'l-Bahá says, "No, no, not that, not that; be happy, be happy," and when one shows enthusiasm and happiness, it seems to lighten His burdens.

The pressure of life there is very great, and sometimes 'Abdu'l-Bahá is very weary, but a quick response to His greeting, or incidents related that show the activity and steadfastness of the believers, will cause His eyes to shine instantly, and His step to become more buoyant. He listens intently to every word, no matter how trifling.

## MORNING SERVICE

Every morning the Holy Family assembled in the Ladies' room for divine service. This was conducted very informally.

Before the chanting 'Abdu'l-Bahá looked over some correspondence, and as the different visitors appeared, tea was offered. The children came and, leaving their sandals outside, knelt near the door, listening quietly. Even the sparrows were welcome, and they flew in and out at their own will (picking up bits of sugar thrown to them by the young girl at the samovar).

Ṭúbá Khánum, Munavvar Khánum, and sometimes the visiting ladies chanted.

One morning 'Abdu'l-Bahá shook hands with us and, turning to the Persian ladies, said, "This looks strange to you, for this is the first time you have seen a man and a woman shake hands. After awhile all will adopt this custom."

Then He asked if the chanting sounded strange to our unaccustomed ears, especially as we could not understand the words. We answered, "Yes." He assented and added that the Persians did not like the "part" singing of the Americans when they first heard it. We told Him that, though we could not understand the words, nevertheless we felt their tremendous power.

He seemed pleased and remarked that if we could

understand them, they would be even more powerful and wonderful to us.

We were reminded of a little incident which happened nine years before.[3] At that time there was a young Syrian girl in the Household who was teaching the Daughters English. She was a Christian and knew nothing of the Bahá'í belief, but one day as we all listened to the chanting, she suddenly burst into tears and ran from the room. They all smiled and quietly awaited her return. In a few minutes she came back, and when asked what made her cry, she shook her head and could only reply, "It was so beautiful—it was so beautiful."

---

The first day at luncheon, after 'Abdu'l-Bahá had partaken of the honey, He passed it to us and said, "Eat this, it will have a spiritual effect—it is the same honey that was offered in the olden time.

"Some material things have a spiritual effect. The spoken words cause a vibration which produces an effect upon the ear. This is material, but the effect is spiritual—that is, the spirit of man feels the effect—either of gladness or sadness."

## THE MASHRIQU'L-ADHKÁR

"To have it built is most important. Some material things have spiritual effect, and the Mashriqu'l-Adhkár is a material thing that will have great effect upon the spirits of the people. Not only does the building of the Mashriqu'l-Adhkár have an effect upon those who build it, but upon the whole world.

"In the time of Christ the believers used a room under a house where they held their meetings. Moses built the Tabernacle. Solomon built the first real Temple.

"In the Mashriqu'l-Adhkár services will be held every morning, and the words of Bahá'u'lláh only are to be read."

Mashriqu'l-Adhkár means "Dawning Point of Mention" (where God is mentioned).[4]

## FEAST

One day a Feast was given for the Persian Jewish pilgrims. Miss M. Elizabeth Jack and we were invited by 'Abdu'l-Bahá to partake of this Feast.

We were conducted to the large hall that was used for these occasions. It was filled with a great variety of growing plants. The table was laden with fruits and cakes, and nine large platters of *pilau,* and beautifully decorated with flowers.

We were placed at the head of the table, then afterward the men-pilgrims appeared. As they came in, one by one, 'Abdu'l-Bahá graciously greeted them and poured water over their hands at a basin. Bashír, 'Abdu'l-Bahá's attendant, held the towel upon which they dried their hands. Afterward they seated themselves at the table.

'Abdu'l-Bahá spoke to Mírzá Munír-i Zayn, who arose and chanted a Tablet. After he finished, 'Abdu'l-Bahá served each one generously to the *pilau.* He walked up and down while the pilgrims ate. When all had finished, 'Abdu'l-Bahá explained that this Feast was for the visiting Jews and said, "In this Great Day, God has manifested One Light, and to this Light are attracted these pilgrims from three great religions — Muḥammadan, Christian, and Jewish. We must all thank God for the privilege of sitting down at this table, for this gathering is a symbol of unity of the Kingdom when all nations, all creeds, all races, and all religions will gather in unity under one Tent, under the shade of one Tree, at one Table to partake of spiritual food."

Then 'Abdu'l-Bahá stood close behind us (three women) and said, "In the olden time, it was not possible for women to sit at table in equality with the men, but in this Day it is different, and the change has been largely brought about by the position given to women in free America.

"It is the power of Bahá'u'lláh that made it possible for these American women to sit at this Table with these pilgrims. This is to show that in the Kingdom of Abhá there will be equality established between women and men. They are equal.

"I am very happy to see you all gathered here, and I hope that the fragrances of this meeting will reach the nostrils of the believers all over the world and make them glad. Such meetings have an effect upon all the people."

After 'Abdu'l-Bahá had finished speaking, the cakes and fruit were partaken of; then the pilgrims arose, and 'Abdu'l-Bahá and those who had assisted Him in serving were seated. Then, in turn, Miss Jack and we were permitted to serve Him and the others, which to us was a great privilege—a wonderful experience.

## SACRIFICE

'Abdu'l-Bahá began by saying that He endured all the pain and hardship of this prison life for the sake of the people, that if it were not for the people He would not stay in a prison. He said, "You should thank God that you are visiting Me in this prison instead of a palace. Most people would like to visit in a beautiful palace, but it is not often that people can visit in a prison." We told Him we knew of many who would love to visit Him in that prison, and that we understood that His was the Great Sacrifice.

He said, "The great Sacrifice is to forget one's self entirely—to sacrifice everything, as did Christ. People might say, 'Why should not God forgive the people without sacrificing His Son?'

"If a king wished to forgive his subjects, would he send his son to be killed by them? Certainly not. If this would be unjust in a king, how much more unjust would it be on the part of God to send His Son to be killed. Christ came of His own will to be a sacrifice that the people might become educated and progress.

"How was He to accomplish this? Must He not give them good counsel; must He not establish new laws and give them new teachings? And if He did all these things, did He not know that the people would rise against Him, give Him great pain and trouble, and finally kill Him? But knowing all this, He was willing to be a sacrifice for the sake of the world, and through this voluntary act He saved all those who believed in Him.

"Christ became a sacrifice that His qualities might appear in the people.

"If God forgave sins without the sacrifice, there would still be only the human qualities in the people. The divine qualities would not appear.

"Christ said to His disciples, 'I am in you, the Father is in Me and I am in you,' meaning that the qualities of the Father were in Him and His qualities were in them.

"There are many explanations of sacrifice. A seed in the ground sacrifices itself—that is, it becomes nothing that the beautiful plant may appear (the qualities of the plant are latent in the seed). The tree and its beautiful branches, leaves, and fruit are manifestations of the perfection of the seed.

"Christ sacrificed Himself, as the seed, becoming as nothing. He produced millions of beautiful trees with their leaves, blossoms, and fruit. The leaves, blossoms, and fruit are manifestations of the perfections that were in the seed, so the disciples became the manifestations of the perfections that were in Christ."

'Abdu'l-Bahá turned to us and said, "As the perfections of Christ appeared in His disciples, I hope, through the Sacrifice of Bahá'u'lláh, His perfections may appear in you." We replied that it would require much of God's mercy to make that possible. He answered, "If you follow His instructions, it is certain to be accomplished."

We told Him what Mr. Chase had said, that while he was at 'Akká he felt that the outside world was the real prison, while 'Akká was the place of freedom.[5] He smiled and said that it was the *freedom* of the world outside that caused Him to be in prison. He said, "This prison is free because of the presence of the Spirit."

## ACCIDENTAL HAPPENINGS

Question: Are there accidental happenings, or do all events occur according to Divine plan?

Answer: God's creation is perfect. Every part of the universe has its connection with every other part, according to a Divine system.

We compare the body of the universe with the body of man. The members of the body of man are closely connected; so, also, are the parts of the great universe. The great events which happen are due to this connection. There is day, there is night; sometimes there are eclipses, etc.—all according to the requirements of this Divine system. All the created beings are connected with each other, and all occurrences and events are indicative of the requirements of this connection and interrelation.

In the body of man, all the members and parts are interdependent; for example, the heart feels the things seen by the eye; the ear hears, and the soul is thereby moved; the nostrils inhale a sweet odor, and the whole body is delighted. This is a proof that all the parts of the body of man are interrelated. This is according to a Divine plan, and it is also evident that there is a great wisdom therein.

Even unpleasant things, such as a chill in the feet which is felt in the head, a disagreeable odor which affects the whole system, or trifles (which are endless, and seem to be accidental) such as a small hair appearing in an unusual place on a man's face, should also be considered as having a place or part in this general system. Therefore, what we call an accident is the effect of the connection of all the parts, and no events transpire in vain.

---

Referring to the Tablet sent to Mr. Dealy previous to the flood and hurricane at Fair Oaks, Alabama: "Be not grieved if the clouds of the Violation of the Covenant are condensed in those regions."

Question: Are great calamities like this flood, the San Francisco earthquake, etc., caused by the wickedness of the people?

Answer: It belongs to the lesson of yesterday. Events like these happen because of the connection between the parts of the universe, for every small part has connection with every great part, and what affects one affects the other or all the others.
On account of this connection, the actions of man have effect. Whenever a promise is broken, it causes a commotion. For instance, suppose two nations have a disagreement. It is a difference in ideas only, and not a physical thing, not anything we can touch or see; yet this disagreement has a physical effect. It causes war, and thousands of men are cut in pieces. So, when man breaks his promise to God, in other words when he "violates the Covenant," the effect is physical, and calamities appear.
A man may be condemned to death because he is a

murderer, another because he is a thief, or they may be punished for many different kinds of crimes, but Jesus Christ was put to death because He wished to become a sacrifice, so there are other causes of calamity.

## THE INCIDENT OF THE DEPARTURE OF MÍRZÁ ASADULLÁH FROM HAIFA AT THE TIME OF THE DISTURBANCE IN 1905

Extract from Mírzá Asadulláh's letter written to the Bahá'ís at that time:

"Our Beloved Master commanded the believers to leave 'Akká for different countries so that they might remain free, but their sorrow at parting from the Master was far greater than would have been the imprisonment. They refused to part with Him, saying they would remain and share with Him His trials. But He admonished them, saying, 'O ye beloved of God. These people (officials) have come especially for Me, and their purpose is not yet known. It is My Will that you should depart from here and serve God wherever you go. This is the appointed time for work; it is the season of victory. If I am crucified or exiled or thrown into the ocean, ye should remain, nevertheless, firm as mountains; nay, your service should become greater and your endurance more. Lay your trust upon God; rest assured in the confirmation of Bahá'u'lláh; spread the Fragrances of God; help the people and lead them to the Light of God. This is the blessed promise of Bahá'u'lláh: "We will help him who rises to serve My Cause through a host of the Supreme Concourse and an army of near angels."'"[6]

"Following the command of the Master, they commenced preparations for their journey. The

Master remained a mountain of firmness, a heaven of patience, and an ocean of steadfastness.

"At this time I was commanded by the Master to go to 'Akká, and reaching there in the afternoon I met the Master and was with Him two hours alone. He gave me directions for teaching, commanding me to go within a few days to Egypt and deliver His Message to the people, telling me He would let me know the time. A few days later my son returned from a visit to the Master and said the time had arrived. On receiving this message, he informed the Master that I had no passport—a necessity in Turkey—to which He replied that I would be protected. The Governor, with his officials, were on the pier to see that no Bahá'í Persons left. As we walked down the pier, the Governor's attention was distracted by the mails which had arrived, and we were enabled to pass to the steamer unnoticed—thus we were protected."

Question: Was this an accidental happening?

Answer: No, this was on account of all the parts of the universe having a connection and being dependent upon one another.

To study the universe, take the body of man; all the elements are in it, and its members are dependent upon one another; so, also, are the parts of the great universe. The great events which happen are due to this connection—all according to the *requirements* of the *system*.

As the great events belong to the general system, so the small things which occur belong to the same Divine system.

In the case of Mírzá Asadulláh, 'Abdu'l-Bahá said, "God told the Governor to turn his head."

Referring to the disturbances at this time, 'Abdu'l-Bahá said, "These things must happen. The clouds will not gather moisture from the sea until the wind blows. Clouds must gather and rain fall and storms appear, or there will be no spring; then we should have no flowers, no fruit, no blessings of Spring. All the happenings in the Cause are for the future fruit."

## BAHÁ'Í ARGUMENT AGAINST THE BELIEF OF THE NATURALISTS REGARDING THE ESSENCE OF GOD OR THE REALITY OF CREATION

We believe in a Universal Essence or Reality, which is purified or exalted above all mention, and which cannot possibly be conceived of by the mind of man. But we can prove Its existence by Its signs which we see in the surrounding creation.

Naturalists believe in this Universal Cause, which they call universal "Nature," and they claim that it, of necessity, brings things into existence, that this necessity is one of the requirements.

We say the Essence is the Creator of all things, and we differ from the Naturalists in attributing the *kind* of qualities to this Essence.

We say that the Essence is purified from all imperfections. They say it has some imperfections.

We say the Essence is conscious.

They say it is unconscious.

We say the Essence is the Knower.

They say it knows not.

We say the Essence has Will.

They say it has no will.

We say the Essence has the power of choice.

They say it creates without choice—because it must.

We prove the existence of the Universal Essence by

qualities that are perfect. They prove the universal "Nature" by qualities that are imperfect.

They say, and try to prove that there is neither organization nor system in the world of existence, that although the works of nature are in themselves perfect (like a flower, for instance) they are not created according to plan or arrangement. For example, in a bouquet of a variety of flowers one sees that each flower, in itself, is perfect, but the arrangement of the bouquet is not according to system.

They say that because the works of nature are not systematic, the Universal Cause can have no consciousness of it.

We ask: Is it possible that perfection can exist in the branch of a tree and not exist in the root of the tree?

Is it possible that perfection shall exist in a drop of the sea and not exist in the sea itself?

Is it possible that perfection will not exist in man himself but will exist in a hair of his head, which is only a part of him?

Is it possible that man, who is a part of the whole, may have qualities of perfection which cannot be attributed to the Essence, or Reality? Or is it possible for man to be a point of perfection and that real Essence be deprived of perfection? A child could not imagine such a foolish thing.

It would also be foolish to say that the hair of a man's head had feeling but that his heart and mind were deprived. (We take the Naturalist's own words for this proof.)

We say that the Essence, or Reality, is purified from all words, all description, and all praise; that the

Essence would have first to be understood and then judged. But man cannot understand the Essence.

The Naturalists say, for example, that the universal "Nature" is like the ocean, and the existent beings are like the waves of that ocean. Now, can we imagine some perfections in the waves without believing that perfection also exists in the ocean itself?

Man is in the position of a little worm in a seed; the seed is in an apple; the apple is on a tree; the tree is in a garden; and the garden is under the care of a gardener.

Now, suppose that little worm should say, "I have understanding and feeling, but the gardener has not." How can this little worm, which is so far from the gardener, possibly have an idea or conception of him? How much could it know of the perfections or qualities of the gardener, so that it might be able to judge whether or not he has such and such perfections, such as consciousness, will, etc.?

The beings in this existent world are created in different conditions. There is the mineral condition, or degree, the vegetable condition, or degree, the animal condition, or degree, and the human degree.

Every higher degree comprehends or includes the lower, but the lower degree does not comprehend the higher. For example, man comprehends the kingdoms below him, but the mineral does not comprehend the three higher kingdoms.

Whatever progress the mineral kingdom may make, it can never reach a condition of knowing the power of growth; and in the same way whatever progress the vegetable kingdom may make, it can never imagine the condition of the animal kingdom; and the animal cannot imagine the human reality.

Though all of them are creations, the difference in degree prevents the lower from comprehending the higher.

As this is so, how can man, the phenomenal being, understand God? How can the creation understand the Creator? How can the art imagine the artist?

Man cannot understand the Reality of Divinity or know whether He has consciousness or not.

The consciousness of God is not the consciousness which we know of. As unconsciousness is an imperfection, we say that Reality has a consciousness. We say so because we want to deny the imperfections ascribed to God. But the consciousness of God is different from the consciousness of man. Man's consciousness is a quality of phenomenal beings, but the consciousness of God is the quality of an Eternal Reality. Therefore, we cannot compare one with the other.

The consciousness of God is sanctified and purified from the consciousness of man.

As it is with the spirit of the vegetable kingdom, which cannot understand the spirit of the animal kingdom or comprehend the sense-perception of the animal kingdom (as an instance, it is impossible for an orange to comprehend the power of sight or to understand the power of hearing or the power of taste), so it is with man, the created being, in his relation to God, the uncreated Reality. It is impossible for him to understand the power of God.

That Reality which is the Essence of God cannot be conceived of by any understanding; therefore, God has created a Manifestor, and in Him is reflected that Sanctified Reality.

The Manifestations are points, or sources, of assistance for all people, and they are the Educators of men. They are like mirrors, and the Reality, the Essence, is like the sun. For instance, the Sun has been reflected by the Mirror of Christ and appears in it with Its Rays and Heat.

Though the Mirror is a phenomenal reality, it is the place of the Sun, or the recipient of the Sun; so, therefore, Christ said, "The Father is in Me," meaning, The Sun has reflected upon this mirror. If the Mirror will say the Sun is in Me—this is right, is truth. But He does not mean that the Sun has come down from Its sanctified height and is dwelling in Him.

In short, we say that man is incapable of understanding the Essence of God and His qualities. Why? Because that Essence is the Highest Sanctity, and man is phenomenal.

## ESSENCE OF THE MATERIAL CREATION

Question: Is the essence of the material creation the Spirit of God?

Answer: No, it is not the *Spirit* of God, but it is the *Bounty* of God. It is not a part of God, for it is His creation.

To illustrate: Take a lamp; its light is created by the sun but is no part of the light of the sun. The action of the sun upon the earth produced the petroleum that gives the light. Neither the petroleum nor the light is any part of the sun.

And so it is with the life, or essence, of all creation.

God has created all beings, but their life, or essence, is not the Life of the Spirit.

The Bounty of God is bestowed upon the mineral, the vegetable, animal, and man, but their life, or essence, is not the Spirit of God.

But when the spirit of man awakens to the consciousness of the Spirit of God and becomes imbued with the Light of the Sun of Truth, that Light in him is of the Spirit of God and is immortal with God. But the man who is not endowed with this Light remains as a lamp whose light may be extinguished.

---

Question: Suppose a man is ill and dies, not having summoned a physician. Had his time come to die, or would he with proper care have recovered?

Answer: There are two kinds of death. One is preordained, and the other is dependent upon many things. For example, a lamp is filled with oil, and it will burn as long as the oil will last. This is preordained. (If the lamp is filled with oil to burn five hours, it will not burn six hours.) Another lamp may be filled, but a strong wind arising may put out the light. This is the other kind of death—dependent upon circumstances.

It is certain that if a babe be thrown into the sea, it will die. This is not preordained death, for the child had just begun its life.

Question: Then these circumstances are somewhat dependent upon the will of man?

Yes, but God has given him that will.

Question: Can any of these circumstances be changed by prayer?

Yes, prayer might prevent the strong wind from blowing out the light of the lamp—but it could never change the amount of oil in the lamp—that is preordained.

---

Question: Do animals have an existence after this life?

Answer: The love shown by animals is instinctive and not dependent upon their own will—that is, they are endowed with their qualities and use them in a natural way, but not by their own will. As these qualities are instinctive and not voluntary, animals will not be rewarded. Their benefits are confined to this world only.

Take a flower; it gives forth a fragrance not of its own will but because it has been naturally endowed. It has no power to withhold the fragrance, so it is compelled to give it out.

This piece of bread gives strength to the body, not by its own will, but because it must. This is of the Bounty of God; therefore, the bread has no reward.

A dog shows affection by instinct and not by will.

A rich man gives a bounty to a poor man. Should the rich man also give him a reward because he has received a bounty? It is the same with the animals. Their qualities are bestowed by God. Shall He give them reward for this Bounty?

Man is the only creature who can receive reward, because he has the power of choice—whether he will show forth love or withhold it. He has the power to choose immortal life or to reject it, while the animals have no qualities that are immortal.

---

For fresh air and exercise we were sometimes permitted to walk on the housetop.

The view from there was superb. Toward the west lay the blue Mediterranean, south of us was the Bay of 'Akká, Haifa, and beautiful Mt. Carmel. To the north and east was the rolling country where the shepherds were tending their sheep as in the olden time, in the same flowing garments, and carrying their shepherds' crooks in the same old way.

From the minarets was heard the call to prayer. How we longed to shout to the muezzin that a "New

Call" had been "vociferously raised" and to the shepherds—the "True Shepherd" hath appeared!

---

At table one day 'Abdu'l-Bahá asked, "If the people here should not let you leave 'Akká, what would you do—how would you feel?"

We answered, "We would stay here always and be perfectly happy." He smiled at this and said, "Suppose they should ask you why you came here? They might say, 'These prisoners are Persians. What have Americans and Persians to say to one another?'"

We answered that we should like nothing better than to mount the housetop and shout to all the people the reason of our coming. He smiled again and said, "You are shouting although you are silent, but your words will be heard in the future. The words of Christ were not heard until three hundred years after His death.

"There is a Persian story of a thief who, in order to rob a certain house, went to work to undermine the foundation. The owner of the house happened to be on the roof and looking down discovered the thief and asked what he was doing. The man replied, 'I am trumpeting.' 'Trumpeting!' exclaimed the owner, 'Why, you are not making any noise.' 'Oh no,' answered the thief, 'you will hear the noise tomorrow!'"

## EVIL THOUGHTS

Question: What is the source of evil thoughts that disturb those who do not wish to entertain them?

Answer: They come from other minds; they are reflected. One should not become a mirror for them—to reflect them; neither should one try to control them, for this is impossible; it only aggravates the difficulty, causing more to appear.

One should constantly turn the mirror of his heart *squarely* toward God so that the Light of the Sun of Truth may be reflected there.

This is the only cure for attacks of evil thoughts. The *face* of the mirror should be turned toward God, and the *back* of the mirror toward the evil thoughts.

---

Question: Are there "earthbound" souls who try to have, and do have, an influence over people, sometimes taking entire possession of their wills?

'Abdu'l-Bahá answered, "There are no earthbound souls. When the souls that are not good die, they go entirely away from this earth and so cannot influence anyone. They are spiritually dead. Their thoughts can have influence only while they are alive on the earth. Caiaphas had great influence during his life, but as soon as he died, his influence ceased. It was of this kind that Christ said, 'Let the dead bury their dead.'

But the good souls are given eternal life, and sometimes God permits their thoughts to reach the earth to help the people."

# AUTOMATIC WRITING

Question: What is the power used in automatic writing?

Answer: This power is neither heavenly nor spiritual; neither is it an influence from disembodied spirits. It is of the human spirit—*magnetism* within the self of the one doing the writing.

When the thoughts have taken possession of the mind and are not consciously directed, one becomes subject to their promptings and, unconsciously, or automatically, takes a pencil and writes them down. The oftener this is done, the stronger becomes the magnetic prompting.

For instance, one may learn a lesson or poem by heart, and he repeats and repeats it so often that the thoughts take possession of him, and he will repeat it unconsciously even in his sleep. This is magnetism belonging to the human spirit.

Or he may walk many times upon a certain road, and he takes his walk so often he is able to take it unconsciously or automatically.

This power is his own magnetism.

A mother rocks and rocks her babe to sleep in a cradle, but the thought of the child's sleep may so take possession of her mind that sometimes she is able to put him to sleep without the aid of the cradle. This effect is produced by the mother's magnetism.

In regard to the automatic writing, if one will pray very earnestly, and pray *sufficiently,* the mind will turn against the automatic writing, and one will be freed from the effects of that power.

Pray, and pray, and not be misled by the seeming beauty of the writings.

---

One of us had a birthday, and 'Abdu'l-Bahá congratulated her upon being in that Sacred Spot for such an anniversary. He was asked to guess the age, and He smilingly guessed several years under the right number. She said, although He was very kind, she was bound to acknowledge a few years more, at which He quickly rejoined, "I wish to make you as young as possible so that you will have so many more years in which to live and spread this Truth." She said that since becoming a Bahá'í, nine years ago, she had been growing younger every day. He smiled and assented, "That is so, and, in reality, you are only nine years old."

Then He told the following story: A great king, walking in his garden one day, noticed a man, about ninety years old, planting some trees. The king asked what he was doing and the old man answered that he was planting date trees. "How long before they will bear fruit?" asked the king. "Twenty years." "But you will not live to enjoy the fruit; why then should you plant these trees?" The old man answered, "The last generation planted trees that bore fruit for my benefit; so it is now my duty to plant for the benefit of the next generation."

The king was pleased at this answer so gave the man

a piece of money. The gardener fell on his knees and thanked him. The king asked, "Why do you kneel before me?" "Because, your majesty, not only have I had the pleasure, or gift, of planting these trees, but they have already borne fruit, since you give me this money." This so pleased the king he gave the man another piece of money.

Again the old gardener knelt, saying, "Again I kneel to thank your majesty. Most trees will bear fruit only once, while these trees of mine have already borne two crops—since you give me two pieces of money."

The king smiled and asked, "How old are you?" The man answered, "I am twelve years old." "How can that be? You are surely a very old man." The gardener answered, "In the days of the king your predecessor, the people were in a most unhappy state of constant warfare and trouble, so I cannot include that as a part of my life. But since your majesty came to rule, the people are happy, contented, and at peace. Therefore, as it is but twelve years since your gracious reign began, I am only twelve years old." This pleased the king so very much that, perforce, he gave the old man another piece of money, saying, "I shall have to leave you now, for your words please me so greatly that if I listen to you longer I shall become a pauper!"

---

One day we spoke of an active worker in this Cause, and 'Abdu'l-Bahá said, "In this Cause, he who is active and who makes an effort will always meet with success. In worldly matters how often we see a man work hard for a lifetime and never achieve success.

But the worker in the cause of God is like a gardener. The more attention he gives his garden, the more fruit will reward his efforts, or, like the traveler who has a great goal before him, no matter how hard the road, if he only keep on walking and is not turned aside by discouragements, he is sure, eventually, to reach his goal."

---

Question: Will the stations of the believers continue to be different hereafter?

'Abdu'l-Bahá answered, "Yes, it will be necessarily so, for the Kingdom requires it.

"The King appoints one to be his prime minister, another to be his greatest general, another a soldier, and so on from the highest to the lowest. If all were generals or all were soldiers, there would be no kingdom.

"God created the mineral, the vegetable, the animal, and man. Had He created only man there would be no world."

## MEMORIAL SERVICE

One of the visiting ladies from 'Ishqábád seemed very sad, and as a sad Bahá'í face is a rarity, we asked about her. It seemed she had lately lost both her daughters within a month's time and was inconsolable.

When she first came, 'Abdu'l-Bahá spent much time comforting her. He told her she must take the believers for her children, and during the days in His Presence, she began to learn real content with God's Will, which is better than resignation. Finally, He revealed some beautiful Tablets for the departed daughters and held a memorial service at which these were read. This was a service of joy and not of sorrow or regret. Only men believers took part in it, but she was able to hear it, although she was not seen. The spiritual effect this blessing had upon her was wonderful to see, and before we left, the empty place in her heart had been filled with His Love, and her face became illumined and beautiful like those of her Persian brothers and sisters.

---

'Abdu'l-Bahá brought us flowers or oranges or grapefruit from the wonderful Riḍván nearly every day and also gave us delicious grapes from a vine that was planted by His own hand. (This vine yields seven crops of grapes every year, and these particular grapes were the seventh yield.)

His constant shower of material and spiritual favors caused us to exclaim that we did not deserve so many blessings, and while we received and received everything from Him, we were unable to give Him anything in return.

He replied, simply, "That is what I am here for—to give, and not to receive."

When we deprecated the trouble it must be to answer so many questions and to give us so much time, He replied, "Whatever is done in love is never any trouble, and—there is always time."

---

'Abdu'l-Bahá entertained the Turkish officials and nonbelievers who came to call nearly every evening. When asked if this was not a great tax on His time and strength, He replied, "Bahá'u'lláh commanded us to show courtesy, kindness, and hospitality to all who come to us—whether they are believers or not." This command 'Abdu'l-Bahá obeyed most conscientiously. Besides showering upon them material favors, He also engaged a man to come and chant the Qur'án, which greatly pleased His Muḥammadan guests.

During the troublous time of 1905 in 'Akká, a Syrian officer in the Turkish army who had always been friendly with the Holy Family, suddenly turned against them. He discovered a book written in English which was detrimental to this Cause. Thinking to ingratiate himself with the powers at Constantinople, he determined to send it there, first having it translated at Beirut. Of course it fell into the hands of the authorities there, who immediately concluded that, since he had the book in his possession, he must himself be a Bahá'í. So they promptly arrested him and sent him to Damascus. Thus he fell into his own trap. But 'Abdu'l-Bahá had no word of censure for this false friend. On the contrary, He, with the Greatest Holy Leaf, went at once to call upon the sorrowful wife, offering her money and every assistance. Here was one of our daily lessons in the practical application of these Great Teachings.

---

In the Words of Paradise page 54, these words appear: "A strange and wonderful instrument exists in the earth, but it is concealed from minds and souls. It is an instrument which has the power to change the atmosphere of the whole earth, and its infection causes destruction."[7]

Question: Does this refer to an evil power such as psychic control? Is there some other power in the world beside God?

Answer: This is a deep and lengthy subject, but, briefly, there is, as we know, a power that composes and a power that decomposes.

The world of existence is constantly revolving through the changes of building up and tearing down.

When elements are attracted, something is composed, and when these same elements are repelled, that form is decomposed.

As by the will of God the power of composition exists, so, also by will of God the power of decomposition exists.

These two are expressed in scripture by 'Isráfíl' the

angel who gives life to men, and the Angel of Death who takes it away.[8] The first is the power of composition or attraction, the other the power of decomposition. They are not angels.

There is no power exercised over the people by those evil souls that have passed away. Good is stronger than evil, and even when alive they had very little power. How much less have they after they are dead, and besides they are nowhere near this planet.

## JOURNEY OF THE ISRAELITES

Question: Was this a physical or spiritual journey?

Answer: It was both physical and spiritual. They journeyed to the Promised Land, and geography and history both prove that this was a physical journey.

Moses viewed the Promised Land, but died before it was reached, having given over his charge to Joshua.

The crossing of the Red Sea has a spiritual meaning. It was a spiritual journey, through and above the sea of corruption and iniquity of Pharaoh and his people, or army. By the help of God, through Moses, the Israelites were able to cross this sea safely and reach the Promised Land (spiritual state), while Pharaoh and his people were drowned in their own corruption.

The Egyptian history recorded even trifling events. Had such a wonderful thing happened as the parting of the physical sea, it would also have been recorded.

---

Question: Christ said, "This generation (meaning dispensation) shall not pass away, till all be fulfilled." (St. Luke 21:32.) And in Ex. 20:5 it states that the sins of the fathers will be visited upon the children unto the third and fourth generation. Does this word generation also mean a cycle, or dispensation?

Answer: No, for the word generation has a different meaning in different places. Christ referred to the

Christ Dispensation, or Cycle, and the other refers to the physical generation.

For example, if a man does a great injustice to another in his life, then, after his death, his son will be despised for having had such a father, and in some cases the injury might be so serious that the effect would reach to the grandson, etc., or a man may, by wrong living, fall into consumption and give that disease to his children unto the third or fourth generation.

Both physically and mentally, the sins of the fathers may be visited upon the children.

---

Question: What was the cause of the Greek Civilization? Did the Greeks ever have a prophet?

Answer: They had philosophers and great men, but while their civilization was full of beauty and was superior to that of the Romans, it was material—neither moral nor spiritual.

The foundation of the Roman civilization was force; consequently, a downfall was inevitable. Think of a monarch like Nero setting fire to a city and playing upon his lyre while it burned! What kind of a civilization was that?

A prophet brings a spiritual civilization, and after that is established, material progress follows.

---

Among the Persian pilgrims who called to see us were several Jews from Hamadán. They were new believers and full of enthusiasm. They told us it made them so happy to behold the American sisters, and they thanked God that they had lived to see the day with their own eyes wherein the prophecies of the Holy Books were fulfilled.

---

Ḥájí Mírzá Ḥaydar-'Alí—that renowned and venerable teacher—said that now he was happy to state there was not a village in Persia, no matter how small, but what contained believers—there might be only one—or ten—or a thousand, but not even the smallest hamlet was without them.[9] We remarked the apparent affinity existing between the Persians and Americans, and the visitors said 'Abdu'l-Bahá had told them that in the future many thousands of Americans would be visiting Persia and many Persians visiting America. This thought seemed to give them all great happiness.

## MIRACLES

One evening Ḥájí Mírzá Ḥaydar-'Alí gave us this little lesson in his inimitably sweet and humorous way.

"If we ask for miracles as proof of the truth of this Revelation, we produce many veils. We should first be sure that the One we believe in has said, 'I am sent by God.' Then if we ask Him for a miracle, for example, to turn this glass cup into gold, He will answer, 'I am sent by God; therefore, I am not against God. God has created this cup out of glass; if I turn it into gold, I am against God.' And not only this; if He perform one miracle to satisfy one person, He will be obliged to perform thousands to satisfy all. Or suppose He should do this for the people who live in His time, what would He have to do to convince those who came after Him? How could He do this? He would have to live forever. Or He would have to divide Himself up and wander all over the earth, knocking at every door and saying, 'I am the Manifestation; what kind of miracles would you like to see?'

"No. Let us see if He comes to improve the condition of the people, to develop their minds and hearts and give them the knowledge of God. If He did turn the cup into gold, what benefit is there in this—what profit or help to the people? Rather He would cloud the intellect and the reason by doing such strange things.

"So we see that the Manifestation cannot follow the desire of the people. He must bring to the world something which all the people can understand, in order that they may recognize that His cause is from God. Now what shall this something be? It is to make the people *understand*. We may say to a man, 'Close your eyes that you may not see,' and he will close them; or 'close your ears that you may not hear,' and he will close them; but when we say 'close your mind that you may not understand,' then that is impossible.

"For example, I may say that I am sure I can wrestle with and overthrow a certain man; the people may declare that I cannot do it; but I am so sure—because I know—that the more they say I cannot, the more positive I become. When a person has learned something like a parrot, as soon as he meets with real opposition he will deny what he has learned; but if *in his own mind* he *understands* the matter, then the more he is opposed, the more sure he becomes. If all the people of the world came and told us that two and two make less than four, would we be disturbed? No, because we understand this matter. When we understand Bahá'u'lláh's Revelation as well as this, then we can stand firm and say to all the world, 'You are wrong, for we are sure.' This kind of understanding only flourishes by opposition.

"When the people asked Christ for a miracle, He declared, 'An evil and adulterous generation seeketh after a sign; and there shall no sign be given to it, but the sign of the prophet Jonas; for as Jonas was three days and three nights in the whale's belly, so shall the Son of man be three days and three nights in the heart of the earth.' The spiritual meaning of these words must be clear. If Christ had performed physical miracles, He would have referred to them instead of giving such an answer; so we must conclude that the miracles were spiritual.

"By saying that He would be three days in the heart of the earth, He meant that He would be resurrected, or reappear in the third cycle or third heaven. Counting His own Dispensation as one, and the Muḥammadan cycle as two, He has reappeared in this, the third Dispensation, the Day of Bahá'u'lláh."

# EXILE OF BAHÁ'U'LLÁH

By Hájí Mírzá Haydar-'Alí

When Bahá'u'lláh was imprisoned in Ṭihrán, the Russian Ambassador went about twenty times to the Sháh to plead in His behalf, saying, "This man has no fault. He is faultless. Why do you imprison Him?" The Sháh answered that Bahá'u'lláh must be punished because He had ordered the attack on his life (see history).[10] The Ambassador said, "That is not a reasonable supposition; for, if He had ordered such an attempt, He would have ordered a bullet put in the gun instead of merely powder and small shot." The Sháh acknowledged this reasoning but was determined to hold Bahá'u'lláh responsible so as to have a pretext for keeping Him in prison.

Again and again the Russian Ambassador went to talk with the Sháh about the matter, and at last the Sháh confessed that he was afraid of the influence of Bahá'u'lláh, and that if he should set Him free, it would create a great tumult among the people.

The Ambassador answered, "If, then, you fear Him so much, why keep Him in Ṭihrán? Would it not be better to exile Him to Baghdád?" This was accordingly done, and an escort furnished of Cossack and Russian horsemen to protect Him from the Persian horsemen. From Baghdád, Bahá'u'lláh was sent to Constantinople, then to Adrianople, then to 'Akká —by force He was sent to the place where He desired to be, thus fulfilling the prophecies of all the Holy Books. He came by His own Will. Had He simply appeared and declared Himself there, the opposers might have said, "Of course, He has read the prophecies and determined to appear in the Holy Land in order to mislead the people." But we see that He used the natural instruments who thought they were sending Him there by force. This is what we may call a real miracle.

After all, did the S̲h̲áh accomplish his will, or did Bahá'u'lláh accomplish His Will?

## KNOWING GOD THROUGH HIS MANIFESTATION OF HIMSELF

Lesson by Ḥájí Mírzá Haydar-'Alí

Both animal and man have material sight, but the animal has no spiritual sight—no power to comprehend spiritual things. And the man who does not accept the revealed Light of God has no conception of the Power of this Light that changes the sight, mind, and heart of those who do accept It.

The Light of God cannot be comprehended by man excepting through His Manifestation. A Christian might search this universe over and over to find God, but he only finds Him when he touches the hem of the Garment of Christ.

In Christ (the Spirit of Truth) we find all spiritual knowledge, all love, all perfection. His perfection is beyond compare. As the ocean is to one drop of water, so is His Perfection above that of the creatures. By comparison all fail to stand in His Presence.

Christ is a Mirror that shows the Essence in Its Perfection. The Essence does not descend to the Mirror, but Its Perfection can be seen in the Mirror, and whosoever loves the Reflection loves the One on High, and whosoever sacrifices himself for this Reflection sacrifices himself for God.

Now, it is certain that God is not realized except through His Manifestation. Now you have recognized

Him, have loved Him, and you have come here to *see Him*. What you have seen, I have seen, and nothing more (meaning that an account of his services in the Cause, which we asked him to relate to us, were as nothing).

The gift God has bestowed upon Bahá'ís can be realized by them, but not by unbelievers. The intellectual power of the whole world cannot understand what power brought Bahá'u'lláh from Ṭihrán to 'Akká.

(In a former lesson H. M. Ḥaydar-'Alí said, "If Bahá'u'lláh had come to 'Akká by Himself—without force—the people might say that anyone could have done the same thing and made the same claim.")

Whatever is done in this world on the material plane, is by means; but The Revelation of God is spread without material means or aid. The Kingdom of God begins here upon earth.

# THE POWER OF GOD

Lesson by Hájí Mírzá Haydar-'Alí

Every matter, whether earthly or heavenly, physical or spiritual—which has not been manifest among men but which has at a certain time become existent—must of necessity be related to one of humankind as its originator, founder, or organizer.

First: If that matter be repugnant to the faith and reason of the world and nations but in accord with their selfish tendencies and desires, it is possible that it may be executed and gain a temporary existence among men, either through the wealth and affluence of its originator or by the means of his power and worldly influence. For people obey and recognize such an unreasonable matter, not only because the worldly power wielded by its originator compels them, but also because that matter appeals to their self-interest and cupidity, though inconsistent with their belief and higher judgment.

Second: If that matter be repugnant to reason but in conformity with faith, it is possible that it may be recognized.

This is illustrated by the doctrine of the Resurrection of Christ and His Ascent to Heaven which, though apparently against reason and science, is still believed in by many without any explanation or proof—because it is the clear, literal text of the Gospels.

Third: And if a matter be contrary to faith but in accord with reason and acquired learning, this can also be established for a time but continues only temporarily, as in the case with the theories of certain philosophers.

Fourth: But if a matter be considered repugnant both to reason and to faith, and be also against men's desire and self-interest, it is utterly impossible for it to be executed and established, even if it is proposed—unless there is an unseen Power to guard and protect it and to establish and promote it in the world. This has been always the case with the Divine Matters—that is the laws and missions of the Prophets and Divine Manifestations. For these Holy Personages executed their commands and promoted their cause among men, although they were alone, unaided, without any family, clan, soldiers, ammunition, or treasures with which to assist and enforce the spread of their Word.

Moreover, they were known as illiterate, unlearned, and were devoid of every worldly means or power. But they fulfilled their mission, made their Cause to triumph, and subjugated nations to their command solely through the power of the greatest Humility and Meekness.

Consequently, the Oneness of God was proven through their Oneness, and the Singleness of God was demonstrated through their Singleness, and from every one of their names and attributes the Divine Names and Attributes became manifest—for they had no worldly instruments, but the Invisible Power of God was their sole Helper, Protector, and Confirmer.

## STORY OF BADÍ'

By Ḥájí Mírzá Ḥaydar-'Alí

This thrilling story of one of the great martyrs in this Cause emphasizes the point that when a man accepts this Truth he becomes a new creature with a new heart and a new character. Badí' was not a particularly good boy—he was very young, and his father, a splendid believer, was somewhat troubled over Badí''s thoughtlessness and carelessness. But when Bahá'u'lláh, declaring Himself from 'Akká to all the rulers of the earth, chose the boy to bear His special Tablet to the Sháh of Persia, Badí' was transformed. Although Bahá'u'lláh told him that when his journey was ended he would be killed, he accepted his mission joyfully.

Concealing the precious Tablet for the Sháh upon his person, he started on foot for Persia. Four months he walked, meeting many believers on the way, but never revealing to anyone his great secret. However, they all noticed that he often turned his face toward 'Akká. He constantly prayed that nothing might hinder him from fulfilling his mission that he might be worthy of the promise of martyrdom. His instructions were that when he reached the capital, Ṭihrán, he was to change his dress and put on a white robe to show that he had no concealed weapon, and station himself outside the gates where the Sháh would ride by with his train. Then he was to hold the Tablet high above his head that all might see what he held. All these things he did, and when the Sháh with his glittering suite came in sight, Badí' raised his hand so that all could see the paper. The Sháh, remarking that he supposed it was a petition from one of his subjects, instructed a soldier to bring it to him. But Badí' called out, "It is not a petition but a command." Instantly the soldiers seized and surrounded him. Again he called to the Sháh, "My Lord, who sent me, told me that you would kill me." The Sháh angrily replied, "We shall not kill you then, just to prove that your Lord does not speak the truth." He ordered that Badí' should be tortured with hot irons and forced to tell all he knew about the Bahá'ís. This was done, but he puzzled the soldiers so that they came to the Sháh saying, "This is a very strange man; the more we torture him, the happier he looks, and he will tell us nothing." This story the Sháh could not believe, so ordered that Badí''s photograph be taken during the torture. It was brought to him showing the smoke rising from the boy's burning flesh and his face more radiant than ever. The Sháh was furious and, forgetting his promise, ordered that Badí' should be killed at once, thus fulfilling the words of Bahá'u'lláh.

About three months later the Sháh asked to see the Tablet which had caused so much trouble, and after reading a few lines was so affected by its power that he threw it from him, exclaiming, "Take it away, for if I read any more, I too shall become a Bahá'í!"

H. M. Ḥaydar-'Alí said: "Bahá'u'lláh endured hardships for the world. 'Abdu'l-Bahá is enduring hardships for the believers that they in turn may give the Light to the world."

---

Mírzá Asadulláh was visiting in 'Akká and came to see us several times. We gave him special messages from some of the American friends, and told him how much the American believers loved him. He smiled, and answered that he loved them very much, for they were all his spiritual children. We also told him how many of his lessons we had copied and spread. He answered, "That is good. But now you have come yourselves to the Fountain—the Source—of all inspiration, and you must take back this Water of Life to all the believers. Here is the Treasure House, and you must fill your hands with jewels to take back to America." We told him that was exactly what we had come for, and hoped our capacity would enable us to take much. He answered, "God also gives the capacity.

"The believers who visit 'Abdu'l-Bahá and go out into the world are like the mists that gather on the bosom of the ocean; soon they will rise and spread, then condense, and shower the precious moisture, thus giving verdure and plenty to all the land."

Mírzá Asadulláh talked most earnestly about the Mashriqu'l-Adhkár, and wished us to tell the believers in America how very, very important it is to have it built now. He said, "Some of the people are poor and so think they cannot help. A few have enough money but think for various reasons they cannot help. But all, each and every one who calls himself a Bahá'í and says the Greatest Name, should have a part in this great work, and if each believer gave only one stone, the building would be finished. It is not to be the home of the people but the Home of God; and while the people are poor, God is rich, and He has commanded that it be built and has promised to help those who arise to obey this command. This prison is now the Home of God; shall we not build in America the finest 'Home of God' possible?"

Among the pilgrims who were delighted to hear of our interest in the Mashriqu'l-Adhkár at 'Ishqábád was Hájí Mírzá Muhammad-Taqí (Afnán), an old, old man who was instrumental in having it built. He is a cousin of the Báb and uncle to Mírzá Muhsin. His work is finished, and he has come to 'Akká to end his days. (All relatives of the Báb's family are called "Afnán.")

---

Mírzá Jináb-i Zayn wrote the *Traveler's Narrative*.[11] He was a devoted follower of Bahá'u'lláh and accompanied Him to Baghdád. When Bahá'u'lláh was sent from there to Constantinople, Mírzá Jináb-i Zayn was exiled alone to Mosul, where he was obliged to stay for twelve years. At last Bahá'u'lláh called him to 'Akká, where he remained until his death—about four years ago. His native town was Najafábád, and when he returned there after an absence, he found but one believer. He taught about five thousand people. When one of his sons died, Bahá'u'lláh comforted him by saying, "You must not grieve over the death of your son; for you have given life to five thousand souls, and they are your spiritual sons." He was also given the name of Zayn, which in Arabic means "good." Two of his sons are now serving 'Abdu'l-Bahá as secretaries—Mírzá Munír-i Zayn and Mírzá Núri'ddín-i Zayn. They very kindly interpreted for us when the Persian pilgrims called and when Hájí Mírzá Haydar-'Alí and Mírzá Asadulláh gave us instruction. Another son of Mírzá Jináb-i Zayn, Mírzá Bushrá Zayn, also interpreted for us.

---

In Cairo, Husayn Rúhí took us to call upon that illumined soul, dear Mírzá Abu'l-Fadl. For some time he had been quite ill but had sufficiently recovered to be able to sit up and renew his writing. When asked about his illness, he said that he did not mind being sick, only that it prevented him from working on the book which 'Abdu'l-Bahá had commanded him to write. He said he was rejoiced to see us and to learn of the progress of the Holy Cause in our country and sent loving greetings to all the American believers.

## INSCRIPTION ON THE GREATEST NAME STONE

"The star is a symbol of man's body (Haykal). The Báb designed the star and wrote 360 forms of the Name of Bahá'u'lláh in the center. These represented the Lights of the Perfection of God which could be contained in the body of a perfect man—Manifestation."

'Abdu'l-Bahá designed the engraving on the stone. The center symbol means the Greatest Name. One star represents the name Báb, and the other star was used to balance the design.[12]

---

Question: Do the hieroglyphics seen inside the great Pyramid refer to Bahá'u'lláh?

Answer: Maybe, but if this is so, it will be known in the future. There are prophecies in the old Persian books that were taken to India long ago by Zoroastrians when they were driven from Persia. In every old gospel, or sacred book, if it be carefully studied, reference to this Day may be found. The old Pársí books are in India, for the Pársís fled to India.

---

Question: Was Confucius a prophet?
Yes, though not so great as Buddha.

---

Question: What is the meaning of verse 52 on page 16 of *The Hidden Words*:

"O Son of Man!"
"My Calamity is My Providence. In appearance it is fire and vengeance; in reality it is Light and Mercy," etc.[13]

Answer: These are the Words of Bahá'u'lláh referring to His persecutions and those of His Martyrs.

---

'Abdu'l-Bahá said: "The form of the cross is made by two lines crossing each other at right angles. It is to be found in everything—even in this piece of cloth. It is the symbol of spiritual sacrifice."

He said: "The present disturbances in Persia remind us of the French Revolution. In time, peace will come. Although the Bahá'ís will make no war in Persia or any other country, the flag of Bahá'u'lláh will overcome every other flag, and all rulers will do homage to it."

---

"You are very fortunate to have come here while there are no disturbances." We answered that we appreciated this blessing and that in His Presence we felt we were at home. He replied, "This is your home.

"You should be very happy to meet the Persian pilgrims in this Holy Place. California and Persia are very far apart, but the pilgrims from the furthermost parts of the earth meet at 'Akká by the power of the Word of God."

---

'Abdu'l-Bahá said He had revealed a Tablet to some Persians in which He wrote that the believers were drops of one sea, rain from one cloud, flowers of one garden, and stars of one heaven.

On His way home from a visit one morning, 'Abdu'l-Bahá noticed a large hawk hovering over the garden. Another had also seen it, and that was a terrified little bird, but when the bird saw Him it flew straight to Him for protection, while the hawk sailed away.

---

One day at luncheon 'Abdu'l-Bahá asked us if we were glad to be at 'Akká and if we were happy. We answered that we were very happy to be there with Him but that when we thought of our faults we were unhappy. He replied *emphatically,* "Think not of yourselves, but think of the Bounty of God. This will always make you happy." Then He smilingly referred to the Arabic saying regarding the peacock, that "He is contented because he never looks at his feet—which are very ugly—but always at his plumage which is very beautiful."

'Abdu'l-Bahá's approbation and encouragement—ignoring one's faults and dwelling on one's virtues—clear the spiritual vision so that, in His Presence, the soul becomes acutely conscious of its own unworthiness. This is God's Way of teaching, and 'Abdu'l-Bahá daily practices the Command, "If a man have ten bad qualities and one good one, look at the one and ignore the ten."[14]

---

Question: Is it necessary to arise to say the midnight prayer, or the prayer of the Dawn, or to wash the hands and face before using these?

Answer: No, the ablution is only for the obligatory daily prayer which should be said three times a day.[15]

Question: Does 'Abdu'l-Bahá wish the believers to take part in charitable or political affairs, or should they interest themselves in spiritual things only?

Answer: Any movement that is for the benefit of mankind should be joined by the Bahá'ís. If they are not asked to help, they should offer their services, especially in all kinds of charitable work. They must not be exclusive but general and serve believers and unbelievers alike. They should also take the usual voter's part in all elections.[16]

## PRONUNCIATION OF BAHÁ'O'LLÁH[17]

The first *a* pronounced as *u* in but.
The second *a* pronounced as *a* in *ah*.
The *o* is a connecting letter and is now used, with the long sound, instead of the connecting letter *u* that all may learn and use the same pronunciation.
Both *ll*s following the *o* are sounded. Slight accent on second and last syllables.

---

Question: Was Bahá'u'lláh a descendant of Cyrus the Great?

Answer: Bahá'u'lláh was a descendant of Abraham.

## MEETINGS

We asked 'Abdu'l-Bahá about our meetings, how they should be conducted, and we told Him we opened our services by saying the Greatest Name nine times in silence. He replied, "That is very good, that is right, for it brings those present into harmony."

Then He said *The Hidden Words* should be read and often the "Tajallíyát"—the Five Holy Tablets—that this was important. *The Hidden Words* are words of counsel, and the "Tajallíyát" are words of instruction, and a preparation for the Kitáb-i-Aqdas. Besides these, other Tablets should be read.

'Abdu'l-Bahá said that discussions and personal opinions expressed had caused inharmony and should be avoided, but that some speaking, such as accounts of the *Visit* by returning pilgrims, etc., always done in love, would be advisable because it was both developing and profitable. In general, it is best that speaking be not confined to one, that the appearance of leadership may be avoided.

"The object of the meetings is to produce harmony and happiness."

'Abdu'l-Bahá highly approved of our dividing into groups for the purpose of answering questions and giving explanations after the service, at teatime. We told Him that the believers took charge of the meetings in turn and that the reading was done in turn, and He also approved of this.

## A MESSAGE SENT BY 'ABDU'L-BAHÁ

### To the Beloved of God

Tell them I love them with all My Heart, that I always think of them and never forget them, that it makes Me happy to hear from them; and when I shall hear that they are *entirely united,* I shall be *perfectly* happy. To become harmonious is very important, for the least inharmony *retards* the bestowal of the great blessings that are awaiting them.

When one or two pilgrims come here, it is the same as if all the members of their assembly were present, and also the same as if all the believers in the world were here; for one or two represent the whole, and when I send My Love and Greetings to the believers through these pilgrims, it is the same as if they were here to receive them, and the Love is the same Love.

I wish the believers could know how much I love them. I would give My Life for them.

# THE PICTURE OF BAHÁ'U'LLÁH

The privilege of viewing the pictures of the Holy Báb and Bahá'u'lláh was accorded us just before we left 'Akká.

This remarkable photograph of the Blessed Beauty is the only one in existence. How perfectly that noble Face and Form embody the Words, "The King has come! The Kingdom and Power, the Glory and Majesty are His! He is the Lord of mankind, the Ruler of the Throne and of the dust!" and at the same time express with such Power the utmost Gentleness and Love.

---

On Saturday morning, the eighteenth of January, after receiving the parting blessing of 'Abdu'l-Bahá and bidding good-bye to all, from the Highest One to the least one in His Service, we drove to that most Sacred Spot, the Rawḍatu'l-Mubáraka, the Holy Tomb of Bahá'u'lláh.

Outside the walls of 'Akká Mírzá Munír joined us, and at the Holy Tomb we were met by Ḥájí Siyyid 'Alí, the brother of Mírzá Muḥsin.

As the resident believers make the pilgrimage on Friday, we had only the company of these two friends. They remained in the inner Court while we entered the Holy of Holies, alone.

That visit is indeed a glorious experience, at once both solemn and joyful.

As we left the heavenly Silence of that Center of Peace, some beautiful roses gathered from the outer garden were given to us, which we gratefully received and have carefully preserved.

From the Holy Tomb we drove to Haifa. Rúḥá Khánum went with us to the Shrine on Mt. Carmel. We saw there the group of trees under which Bahá'u'lláh loved to rest.

## SYMBOLIC PICTURE

As we slowly descended Mt. Carmel our eyes beheld a *symbolic picture* of wondrous beauty.

Before us spread the Bay of 'Akká. The sun had just disappeared (to our left), and it was still daylight, the glowing colors of the sky and landscape remaining.

To our right stretched the cream-colored beach; and, beyond, the dark green line of shrubs and trees followed its curve.

Still further on was the range of blue mountains, snowcapped.

The full moon of orange color had already risen above these mountains, and its golden beams reached across the bright blue Bay.

Directly opposite lay 'Akká, the Beautiful, its forlorn, ancient buildings transfigured in that wonderful light to marble palaces, carved and jeweled—a "White City" rising from the Bay, its domes and minarets pointed with rubies.

The following Words of Bahá'u'lláh interpret the symbol:

"O people of the earth! When the Sun of My Bounty sets and the Firmament of My Form is hidden, be not troubled. Arise for the helping of My Work and the advancement of My Word throughout the world. Verily, We are with you under all conditions and will help you with the Truth."[18]

"Say, O people!

"Let not trouble take possession of you when the kingdom of My Epiphany becomes concealed and the waves of the Ocean of My Utterance are hushed.

"Verily, there is in My Epiphany a reason and in My *Occultation* another reason which none knoweth save God, the Incomparable, the All-Knowing.[19] And we shall see you from the most Glorious Horizon and will help whosoever riseth up for the helping of Our Work with hosts from the Supreme Concourse and a cohort of the Cherubim."[20]

At the time of the disappearance of the "Form" of the "Sun" (Bahá'u'lláh), the "Moon" of this Dispensation ('Abdu'l-Bahá) had already arisen, and the Beams of this "Orb of peace and reconciliation" have encircled the globe.

As the light of the material sun remains long after it has set, so, in this Day, the Light of the Sun of God's Manifestation remains, and the "Moon" of this Manifestation, being so high in the spiritual heaven, above the earthly states and conditions, will continue to reflect in greatest splendor the Light of the Heavenly Sun.

---

On the nineteenth of January we left the Holy Land, our spiritual Home, to enter the world again. Our hearts were full to overflowing with the gracious gifts which had been bestowed—not only upon us, but upon all the friends to whom we were bearing 'Abdu'l-Bahá's loving messages.

---

As we sailed away, gazing at 'Akká, it presented a different appearance from its material reality. Instead of a crumbling, gray stone building, the prison, as it projected into the blue Sea, looked like an exquisite white marble "casket."

From the worldly standpoint, it is truly a prison. From the heavenly standpoint, it is truly a "Casket" containing

THE GEM OF MYSTERY, 'ABDU'L-BAHÁ.

# APPENDICES

APPENDIX I

## TABLET TO MRS. ELLA GOODALL COOPER

*Through his honor
Mírzá Aḥmad and Mírzá Munír.
Translated by M. A. Iṣfahání, Sept. 29, 1908.*
To the maidservant of God,
Mrs. Ella Goodall Cooper.
Upon her be Bahá'u'lláh-al-Abhá!

HE IS GOD!

Oh, thou who art attracted to the Kingdom of God!

Thy detailed letter was received. Its perusal produced the utmost happiness, for it evidenced the fact that thou hast attained to the knowledge of the reality of tests, that tests endured in the Path of God are conducive to confirmation, nay, rather, they are heavenly powers and the bounties of the realm of Might. But to the weak believers tests are trials and examination, for, on account of the weakness of their faith and assurance, they fall into difficulties and vicissitudes.

However, to those souls who are firm and steadfast, tests are the greatest favors.

Consider thou that at the time of an examination in sciences and arts, the dull and lazy pupil finds himself in calamity. But to the intelligent and sagacious student, examination in learning produces honor and infinite happiness. Alloyed gold subjected to the fire portrays its baseness, while the intensity of the flame enhances the beauty of pure gold. Therefore, tests to the weak souls are calamity, and to the veiled ones the cause of their disgrace and humiliation.

The point is this, that in the Path of Truth every difficulty is made plain and every trial is the matchless bounty.

Therefore, the believers of God and the maidservants of the Merciful must not relax during trial, and no disaster must deter their service in the Cause of God.

You have written that upon your return you have compiled whatever you saw and heard (at 'Akká) and you have received the invisible assistance, that the teachings, which were like invisible seeds, have sprung to life and verdancy, spreading branches and leaves, and producing blossoms and fruits. Indeed, what you have written is true.

You have asked regarding the influence of evil spirits. Evil spirits are deprived of eternal life. How then can they exercise any influence? But as *eternal life* is ordained for holy spirits, therefore their influence exists in all the divine worlds.

At the time you were here, this question was accordingly answered, that after the ascension of the godly souls, great influence and widespreading bounties are destined for them, and all-encircling signs in the seen and unseen are decreed for them.

When the souls leave the bodies, they do not assume elemental bodies. Whatever man thinks regarding this is but his own imagination.

When man desires help and communication from holy souls, he puts himself in a condition of self-unconsciousness and becomes submerged in the sea of meditation, then a spiritual state, which is sanctified from matter and all material things, becomes visible and apparent to him. Then he thinks he beholds a form. Its appearance is like unto a vision.

Man beholds in the world of vision various images, communicates with them, and receives benefits, and in that world of vision he *thinks* they are physical temples and material bodies, while they are purely *immaterial*.

Briefly, the reality of the soul is sanctified and purified above matter and material things, but like unto the world of vision, it manifests itself in these material forms and visages. Likewise, in the psychic condition, one beholds the spirits like unto physical forms and visages.

To be brief, the holy souls have great influence and intense effect, and their influence and continuity does not depend upon physical existence and elemental composition.

Ponder ye, that during sleep the human body and the five physical senses, viz., sight, smell, taste, hearing, and touch are passive—i.e., all physical forces are inactive. Notwithstanding this, human reality has spiritual life, and the spiritual powers are penetrative; and wonderful disclosures are made in both the East and the West, and perchance one may discover some matters, which, after a long time, may become apparent in the physical world. Therefore, it has become evident that the continuity and influence of the human reality does not depend upon the physical instrumentality; nay, rather, the physical body is an instrument over which the human spirit spreads a luminosity. It is like unto the sun which, shining upon the mirror, causes its brilliancy, and when the reflection is withdrawn from the mirror, it becomes dark. Likewise, when the luminosity of the human spirit is withdrawn from the body, that instrument becomes useless.

To be brief, Humanity consists of the spiritual reality, and that reality is penetrative in all things, and it is that reality which discovers the invisible mysteries, and through that reality all sciences, arts, and inventions become known and manifest. Whatever thou beholdest of the works of man is but a faint ray of *that* reality. It encircles all things and comprehends all things.

Reflect thou that all these existent sciences, crafts, industries, and arts were at one time in the world of invisibility, unknown and concealed mysteries. As the spirit of man environs all things, therefore he has discovered them and brought them from the unknown world into the arena of manifestation.

Therefore, it is evident and established that the human spirit is the discoverer of things, the seer of things, and the comprehender of things.

But regarding the progress of the spirit in the world of the Kingdom after its ascension, it is wholly beyond space and time, and developments after leaving this body are spiritual and not terrestrial. It is like unto the progress of the child from the world of the fetus to the world of maturity and intelligence, from the world of ignorance to the world of knowledge, from the station of imperfection to the pinnacle of perfection.

As Divine Perfections are infinite, therefore the progress of the spirit *is limitless.*

Whatever the European and American historians have written regarding His Highness Muḥammad the Messenger of God, most of it is falsehood.

Consider ye, is it possible for a person afflicted with epilepsy to establish such a great nation?

Therefore, this statement of the European historians regarding that Holy Personage is unqualified falsehood.

Reflect ye that that Illustrious Personage was born in the Sahara of Arabia among the ignorant tent dwellers, affiliating and associating with them till he grew to manhood and maturity, never studying the sciences and arts; nay, even He was apparently illiterate and uninstructed. Notwithstanding all this, He brought forth such a nation, established such a religion, and uttered such explanations regarding scientific questions, with great perspicuity, and raised such a community from the nadir of ignorance and barbarism to the zenith of civilization and prosperity! Through His influence, science, literature, philosophy, crafts, and trades made wonderful progress during the medieval ages in Andalusia and Baghdád.

Now is it possible that such an illustrious Personage be afflicted with epilepsy?

Relative to the Paradise explained by Muḥammad in the Qur'án, such utterances are spiritual and are cast into the mold of words and figures of speech; for at that time people did not possess the capacity of comprehending spiritual significances. It is similar to that reference to His Highness Christ who, addressing His disciples said, "I shall not partake of the fruit of the vine anymore until I reach the Kingdom of My Father." Now it is evident His Highness Christ did not mean material grapes, but it was a spiritual condition and a heavenly state which He interpreted as this fruit.

Now, whatever is revealed in the Qur'án has the same import.

Regarding the Most Great Name, Its influence, both in physical and spiritual affairs, is indisputable and certain.

In the last Tablet (to the Board of Council of New York) in which I have stated, "I am not Christ and am not eternal," the meaning is this, that I am not Christ—and not the Eternal Lord! But I am 'Abdu'l-Bahá. This is its real purport. Undoubtedly, those souls who are under the shadow of the Blessed Cause, believing and assured, firm and steadfast, and living in accord with the Divine exhortations and advices, all of them are confirmed in the Everlasting Life.

Regarding the materialization of spirits through mediums: A person finding himself in a state of trance, or unconsciousness, is like one who sleeps; whatever he feels and sees he imagines to be matter and of material things, but in reality they are *wholly immaterial*.

O thou maidservant of God! Arouse ye the people and make them cheerful through the Glad Tidings of God, and quicken them through the Spirit of Gladness and Heavenly Rejoicing. The essence and foundation of all is to advance toward the Kingdom of Abhá and to be attracted by the Beauty of God. Whatever produces any influence in the world of existence is on account of the Love of God, which is the Spirit of Life and the cause of Salvation.

Convey on behalf of 'Abdu'l-Bahá wonderful Abhá Greetings to the believers and the maidservants of the merciful.

Upon thee be Bahá'ul-Abhá!
(signed) 'ABDU'L-BAHÁ 'ABBÁS

APPENDIX II

# TABLET TO MRS. ELLA GOODALL COOPER[21]

*Through Dr. Amínulláh Faríd.*
To the revered Maidservant of God,
Mrs. Ella G. Cooper.
Upon her be Bahá'u'lláh!

## HE IS GOD!

O thou who art attracted to the Kingdom of God: Thy writing of August 19, 1905, was considered, and the contents were a source of joy.

If thou question regarding the trials and difficulties of 'Abdu'l-Bahá, that is a sea, boundless, surging, and full of storms; but 'Abdu'l-Bahá is in perfect peace and composure, and in complete joy, happiness, and tranquility; nay, it is for Him a ready banquet and an adorned feast. I hope that at the end of this feast and banquet the overflowing chalice of Martyrdom will come round to Him, and then will He be intoxicated by that wine.

But you must not look to the catastrophes of 'Abdu'l-Bahá. Consider power and strength, and withstand the world. For the sake of 'Abdu'l-Bahá bear the persecution of the enemies, and the blame of those who oppose. Under all conditions, My Soul and My Life shall abide with you in this world as well as the world above.

O maidservant of God! Hasten and sow the seed as

best you can, for time passes away, and through it shall the blessing of the Kingdom appear.

Question: Is astrology a real science, and is it possible for persons to receive messages or trumpet communications from departed souls, etc.?

O, thou maidservant of God! There is a wonderful power and strength which belongs to the human spirit, but it must receive confirmation from the Holy Spirit. The rest of which you hear is superstition. But if it is aided by the Bounty of the Holy Spirit, it will show great power; it will discover realities; it will be informed of the mysteries. Direct all the attention to the Holy Spirit, and call the attention of every soul to It. Then will you see wonderful signs.
O maidservant of God! The planets and stars have no spiritual effect in the earthly world, but the parts of the universe which are in endless space are closely connected with each other. This connection produces material effects. Outside of the Bounty of the Holy Spirit all that thou hearest concerning mesmerism or trumpet communications from the dead are sheer imagination.
But thou canst say whatever thou desirest concerning the Bounty of the Holy Spirit, and what thou hearest from the Holy Spirit and obey. But the people who are mentioned, those in connection with the trumpets, are entirely bereft of this Bounty, and they have no portion therein. Theirs is imagination.

Question: Are prayers answered by the Essence of God or by His Manifestation?

O, thou maidservant of God! The answer to prayer is through the Great Manifestation of God. But for obtaining material things, if the ignorant (of the Manifestation) supplicate and implore and pray God, it will also be effective.

O, thou maidservant of God! Although the Reality of Divinity is boundless, yet the purposes and needs of the servants are limited. The Bounty of God is like unto the rain from Heaven. The water has no limit and no form, but in every place it will take to itself a form and effect peculiar to the capacity and preparation thereof. That shapeless water when poured into a square reservoir will appear as a square. Likewise when in the hexagonal vessel or in the octagonal. Water has no geometry, no limit, and no form. But it will appear in one of the forms according to the exigencies of time and place.

Likewise the Holy Essence of God is boundless, but Its Manifestation and Bounty in the creatures is limited. Thus the prayers of certain persons concerning special matters are answered accordingly.

Question: Were the Healing Tablets intended for physical healing or only spiritual illness?

O maidservant of God! The prayers which were written for the purpose of healing are both for the spiritual and material healing. Therefore, chant them for the spiritual and material healing. If healing is best for the patient, surely it will be granted. For some who are sick, healing for them shall be the cause of other ills. Thus it is that Wisdom does not decree the answer to some prayers.

O maidservant of God! The power of the Holy Spirit heals both material and spiritual ills.

Question: It is claimed by some Bible students that the Valley of Achor, referred to in Hosea 2:15, does not mean the City of 'Akká, and is not a prophecy relating to this Manifestation. Is this another place?

O maidservant of God! It is recorded in the Bible: "Achor shall be a door of hope unto them." This Achor is the City of 'Akká. Whosoever interprets this otherwise is ignorant.[22]

O thou maidservant of God! I hope that thou mayest again make the pilgrimage to this Blessed Spot and attain great development.

Question: Was Buddha a real prophet sent by God?

O thou maidservant of God! Buddha was also one of the prophets, but His teachings were interpolated and altered. What the Buddhists now have in hand is contrary to the original laws of Buddha.
Upon thee be greetings and praise,
    (signed) 'ABDU'L-BAHÁ 'ABBÁS

*Translated by Amínulláh Faríd, December 30, 1905.*

APPENDIX III

## TABLET PREDICTING THE "TESTS" OF SAN FRANCISCO.

To the Maidservant of God,
Mrs. Helen S. Goodall—California.
Upon her be Bahá'u'lláh!

HE IS GOD!

O thou who art attracted to the Fragrances of God!
Verily, I read thy latest letter, and My great love welled forth unto thee on account of its wonderful contents. Verily, it showed thy firmness in the Cause of God, and that thou wilt resist great tests in the future. *Still greater tests will appear in your great city.*

As to thee, make firm the footsteps of the believers of God on this right Path, and say, verily, the test has a great power, and when its storms wax fierce, they uproot everything, even large and well-rooted trees, and they wreck great ships on the ocean.

But whoso among the maidservants of God firmly resists a great test, her face shall gleam, and her brow shall glitter in the Supreme Concourse. This is what We inform thee, so that when the test appears, thou mayst be heedful thereof and mayst remind the maidservants of God that the tests have also occurred in former dispensations, even at the time of Christ.

Christ said, "Fast, so that you may not fall into temptation." Verily, tests withheld a great apostle

(Judas) from the Mercy of God and made him take part in the shedding of the Christ's blood. The tests made Peter the apostle deny Christ. The tests made the brothers of Christ deny Him. Many a just, faithful, and assured soul did not endure the power of the tests, turned backward, until they reached the lowest of the low.

O maidservant of God! Rely upon the Bounty of thy Master, for, verily, thou art firm and steadfast, and His Favor is great and great toward thee. But make firm the hearts of the maidservants and believers in this Cause, which the greatest powers of the world cannot withstand, and which spreads in spite of all through the Power of the Kingdom of God.

Upon thee be greeting and praise.

(signed) 'ABDU'L-BAHÁ 'ABBÁS

*Translated by Ali-Kuli Khan, April 16, 1902.*

APPENDIX IV

## PORTIONS OF TABLETS SENT BY 'ABDU'L-BAHÁ

To Mrs. Helen S. Goodall.

*Translated by Anṭún F. Ḥaddád.*

In *The Hidden Words* "Leave the ego" means that man must leave his passions and lusts, his human sentiments, his personal interests and aims, and seek the Spiritual Fragrances and Heavenly Attractions, and become drowned in the sea of redemption, and drawn to the Beauty of Al-Abhá.[23]

In *The Hidden Words* "Remember the covenant you entered into with Me upon the Mount of Paran" means that in relation to the Truth (God) the past, the present, and the future are regarded as one time, but in relation to the created beings, the past has passed and expired, the present is about vanishing, and the future is the place of hopes.[24]

Of the fundamental principles of the Law of God, there is one which means that in every Prophetical Mission God taketh a covenant from all the souls which come up to the end of that mission, which is the Promised Day of the Appearance of a Promised Person.

Look back to Moses, the Interlocutor. Verily, He took the Covenant of Christ upon the Mount of Sinai from all the souls who came in the time of Christ. Those souls, though they came after Moses by ages and generations, yet, with reference to the Covenant which is sanctified from times, they were present. But the Jews were heedless and did not remember; so they fell into a manifest loss.

In the Arabic *Hidden Words* "No peace was ordained for thee save by cutting the ego from thyself": It means that man, also, must not seek for himself in this perishable world anything, but must be separated from it—i.e., he must redeem his whole soul under all conditions, in the place of martyrdom, on the appearing of its Lord.[25]

*Through Dr. Amín Faríd, January, 1903.*

As to thy question concerning the "Minor Resurrection" and the first creation, this is the appearance of the Báb, the Great, His Holiness the Supreme. But the "Major Resurrection" signifies the Manifestation of the Preexistent Beauty (Bahá'u'lláh), the GREATEST NAME. (May My Spirit be a sacrifice for His beloved!)

By the majesty of My Lord, your gathering in the meeting of Oneness, your commemoration of God with a pure heart, and your association with a spirit rejoiced by the Spirit of God in the Great Day profiteth you more than all favors and this Bounty surpasseth all wishes.

O maidservant of God, assemble the maidservants of the merciful with all spirituality and fragrance, love and attraction, and raise your voice in the praise and glory of your Majestic Lord for His abundant mercy and great favor of guidance.

Upon thee be greeting and praise.

(signed) 'ABDU'L-BAHÁ 'ABBÁS

ALLÁH-U-ABHÁ!

# NOTES

# NOTES

1. For a more accurate translation see Bahá'u'lláh, *The Hidden Words of Bahá'u'lláh*, trans. Shoghi Effendi (Wilmette, Ill.: Bahá'í Publishing Trust, 1939), p. 48.—ED.

2. Marion Elizabeth Jack (1866–1954) taught English to 'Abdu'l-Bahá's grandchildren in 'Akká in 1908. In response to the Tablets of the Divine Plan she taught the Faith of Bahá'u'lláh in many places in North America and pioneered to Alaska and later to Bulgaria for the last twenty-four years of her life. On her death Shoghi Effendi called her an "immortal heroine," and a "shining example (to) pioneers (of) present and future generations. . . ." See "In Memoriam: Marion Jack," *The Bahá'í World: A Biennial International Record, Volume XII, 1950–1954*, comp. National Spiritual Assembly of the Bahá'ís of the United States (Wilmette, Ill.: Bahá'í Publishing Trust, 1956), pp. 674–77.—ED.

3. Ella Goodall Cooper here recalls an experience from her first pilgrimage to Haifa in 1898–99.—ED.

4. Mashriqu'l-Adhkár is more accurately translated "The Dawning Place of the Praise of God." See [The Universal House of Justice], "Notes and References," in Bahá'u'lláh, *A Synopsis and Codification of the Kitáb-i-Aqdas: The Most Holy Book of Bahá'u'lláh*, [comp. The Universal House of Justice] (Haifa: Bahá'í World Centre, 1973), p. 61.—ED.

5. Thornton Chase (1846–1912), who became a Bahá'í in Chicago in 1894, was the first believer in America and the Western world. For more information see Mirza Ahmad Sohrab, "Abdul-Baha at the Grave of Thornton Chase: Los Angeles, California, October 19, 1912," *Star of the West*, 3, no. 13 (Nov. 4, 1912), 14–15, and O. Z. Whitehead, *Some Early Bahá'ís of the West* (Oxford: George Ronald, 1976), pp. 1–12.—ED.

6. For a more accurate translation see Bahá'u'lláh, *Gleanings*

from the *Writings of Bahá'u'lláh*, trans. Shoghi Effendi, 2d rev. ed. (Wilmette, Ill.: Bahá'í Publishing Trust, 1976), p. 139.—ED.

7. For a more accurate translation see Bahá'u'lláh, *Tablets of Bahá'u'lláh Revealed after the Kitáb-i-Aqdas*, comp. Research Department of the Universal House of Justice, trans. Habib Taherzadeh et al. (Haifa: Bahá'í World Centre, 1978), p. 69.—ED.

8. According to Islám, on the Day of Judgment Isráfíl calls the dead to rise to a new life.—ED.

9. Hájí Mírzá Haydar-'Alí of Isfahán was a devoted servant of the Báb, Bahá'u'lláh, and 'Abdu'l-Bahá from the 1850s to his death in 1920. At Bahá'u'lláh's bidding he went to Egypt to teach about the Bahá'í Faith; his efforts resulted in his being imprisoned for nearly ten years. For more than twenty-five years he was one of the foremost teachers in Persia; he staunchly defended the Covenant of Bahá'u'lláh at His passing and during 'Abdu'l-Bahá's ministry. He spent the last years of his life as companion to 'Abdu'l-Bahá and counselor to pilgrims; the Western pilgrims knew him as the Angel of Mount Carmel. For details on his life see Adib Taherzadeh, *The Revelation of Bahá'u'lláh: Adrianople 1863–68* (Oxford: George Ronald, 1977), pp. 438–50.—ED.

10. It is not clear to what "see history" refers; perhaps it means to see historical accounts of the August 12, 1852, attempt on the life of the Sháh.—ED.

11. According to H. M. Balyuzi (*Edward Granville Browne and the Bahá'í Faith* [London: George Ronald, 1970], p. 10n), "A manuscript copy [of *A Traveler's Narrative*] in the handwriting of an eminent Bahá'í, Zaynu'l-Muqarribín [Jináb-i Zayn], was given to Browne in Bahjí, 'Akká, in 1890. This book was written by 'Abdu'l-Bahá, but at that time its authorship was anonymous. Browne had that manuscript published in facsimile. . . ." Probably Mrs. Goodall and Mrs. Cooper were told that Jináb-i Zayn wrote *A Traveler's Narrative* in the sense that he copied it; they may have misunderstood and thought that he had authored it. For accounts of Jináb-i Zayn's life and work see 'Abdu'l-Bahá, *Memorials of the Faithful*, trans. Marzieh Gail

(Wilmette, Ill.: Bahá'í Publishing Trust, 1971), pp. 150–53, and Adib Taherzadeh, *The Revelation of Bahá'u'lláh: Baghdád 1853–63* (Oxford: George Ronald, 1974), pp. 25–26.—ED.

12. For a detailed explanation of the Greatest Name see Abu'l-Qásim Faizi, "Explanation of the Emblem of the Greatest Name" (Wilmette, Ill.: Bahá'í Publishing Trust, 1977), reprinted from *Bahá'í News*, no. 451 (Oct. 1968), pp. 8–12.—ED.

13. When Shoghi Effendi translated *The Hidden Words*, he renumbered the Arabic section. For his translation see Bahá'u'lláh, *Hidden Words*, p. 15, no. 51.—ED.

14. For a more accurate translation see 'Abdu'l-Bahá, quoted in J. E. Esslemont, *Bahá'u'lláh and the New Era: An Introduction to the Bahá'í Faith*, 3d rev. ed. (Wilmette, Ill.: Bahá'í Publishing Trust, 1970), p. 83.—ED.

15. The Medium Obligatory Prayer is to be recited three times daily, in the morning, between noon and sunset, and in the evening. The Short Obligatory Prayer is to be recited once in twenty-four hours, between noon and sunset. The Long Obligatory Prayer is to be recited once in twenty-four hours. According to Shoghi Effendi, "The daily obligatory prayers are three in number . . . The believer is entirely free to choose any one of those three prayers, but is under the obligation of reciting either one of them, and in accordance with any specific directions with which they may be accompanied." Shoghi Effendi, quoted in Bahá'u'lláh, The Báb, and 'Abdu'l-Bahá, *Bahá'í Prayers: A Selection of the Prayers Revealed by Bahá'u'lláh, The Báb, and 'Abdu'l-Bahá*, rev. ed. (Wilmette, Ill.: Bahá'í Publishing Trust, 1970), pp. 117–28. For further details on obligatory prayers and a description of ablutions see Bahá'u'lláh, *Synopsis and Codification*, pp. 35–37.—ED.

16. According to The Universal House of Justice, "If a Bahá'í works for one political party to overcome another it is a negation of the very spirit of the Faith. Membership in any political party, therefore, necessarily entails repudiation of some or all of the principles of peace and unity proclaimed by Bahá'u'lláh. As 'Abdu'l-Bahá stated: 'Our party is God's party; we do not belong to any party.'" The Universal House of Justice, *Messages from The*

*Universal House of Justice: 1968–1973* (Wilmette, Ill.: Bahá'í Publishing Trust, 1976), p. 46. See also Shoghi Effendi, *The World Order of Bahá'u'lláh: Selected Letters*, 2d rev. ed. (Wilmette, Ill.: Bahá'í Publishing Trust, 1974), pp. 64–67, and "Membership Criteria in Non-Bahá'í Groups" in *National Bahá'í Review*, no. 106, (Feb. 1978), p. 5.—ED.

17. The correct transliteration is Bahá'u'lláh.—ED.

18. For a more accurate translation see Bahá'u'lláh, *Synopsis and Codification*, p. 14.—ED.

19. Occultation means absence from the physical world. Shoghi Effendi translates this line as follows: "In My presence amongst you there is a wisdom, and in My absence there is yet another, inscrutable to all but God, the Incomparable, the All-Knowing." Bahá'u'lláh, *Gleanings*, p. 139.—ED.

20. For a more accurate translation of the entire passage see ibid.—ED.

21. For a more accurate translation of excerpts from this Tablet see 'Abdu'l-Bahá, *Selections from the Writings of 'Abdu'l-Bahá*, comp. Research Department of the Universal House of Justice, trans. Committee at the Bahá'í World Centre and Marzieh Gail (Haifa: Bahá'í World Centre, 1978), pp. 160–62.—ED.

22. The Universal House of Justice in a letter dated February 20, 1978, to the National Spiritual Assembly of the Bahá'ís of the United States, noted that, "There is a Tablet written by 'Abdu'l-Bahá to an individual believer in California on 19 August 1905 in which He states, 'In the Torah it says that the Valley of Achor was made for you a door of hope; this valley is the city of 'Akká, and this is certainly so . . .'. This is similar to the statement of the Guardian on page 184 of "God Passes By", 'Akká, itself, . . . designated by Hosea as a door of hope'. . . . it is thus made indisputably clear that the Valley of Achor (which means Valley of Trouble) in this prophecy refers to the City of 'Akká. . . ."—ED.

23. Shoghi Effendi translates this phrase as "Renounce thyself." See Bahá'u'lláh, *Hidden Words*, p. 35, no. 38.—ED.

24. For a more accurate translation see ibid., p. 46.—ED.

25. For a more accurate translation see ibid., p. 5.—ED.